# MUSIC MINUS ONE TROMBONE

## PACIFIC COAST HORNS

V O L U M E   3

# Where Trombone Reigns

3977

# SUGGESTIONS FOR USING THIS MMO EDITION

W<small>E HAVE TRIED</small> to create a product that will provide you an easy way to learn and perform these compositions with a full ensemble in the comfort of your own home. The following MMO features and techniques will help you maximize the effectiveness of the MMO practice and performance system:

Because it involves a fixed accompaniment performance, there is an inherent lack of flexibility in tempo. We have observed generally accepted tempi, and always in the originally intended key, but some may wish to perform at a different tempo, or to slow down or speed up the accompaniment for practice purposes; or to alter the piece to a more comfortable key. For maximum flexibility, you can purchase from MMO specialized CD players & recorders which allow variable speed while maintaining proper pitch, and vice versa. This is an indispensable tool for the serious musician and you may wish to look into purchasing this useful piece of equipment for full enjoyment of all your MMO editions.

We want to provide you with the most useful practice and performance accompaniments possible. If you have any suggestions for improving the MMO system, please feel free to contact us. You can reach us by e-mail at *info@musicminusone.com*.

mmo
3977

# CONTENTS

MMO 3977

4

Trombone

# Alexander's Ragtime Band

By IRVING BERLIN
Arrangement by PAUL CHAUVIN

**7**

Trombone

# The Toy Trumpet

Music by RAYMOND SCOTT
Arrangement by CHARLES WARREN

**V.S.**

MMO 3977

Trombone

# Stompin' at the Savoy

Words by ANDY RAZAFF
Music by BENNY GOODMAN, EDGAR SAMPSON
and CHICK WEBB
Arrangement by PAUL CHAUVIN

Trombone

The Original, First and Foremost Version of:
# The Blue Danube

the mistake waltz
by JOHANN STRAUSS, JR.
Arrangement by PAUL CHAUVIN

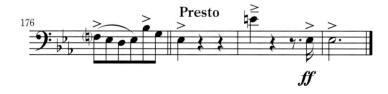

Trombone

# Mysterious Mose

Words and Music by
WALTER DOYLE and TED WEEMS
Arrangement by CHARLES WARREN

MMO 3977

Trombone

# Harlem Nocturne

Words by DICK ROGERS
Music by EARLE HAGEN
Arrangement by PAUL CHAUVIN

Trombone

# Bugle Call Rag

by JACK PETTIS, BILLY MYERS
and ELMER SCHOEBEL
Arrangement by CHARLES WARREN

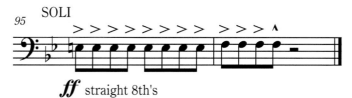

Trombone

# Les Toreadors

from CARMEN

By GEORGE BIZET
Arrangement by CHARLES WARREN

MMO 3977

# Caravan
## from SOPHISTICATED LADIES

Trombone

Words and Music by
DUKE ELLINGTON, IRVING MILLS
and JUAN TIZOL
Arrangement by PAUL CHAUVIN

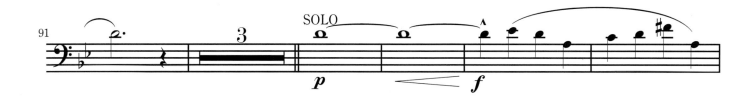

Trombone

# Blue Rondo A La Turk

By DAVE BRUBECK
Arrangement by CHARLES WARREN

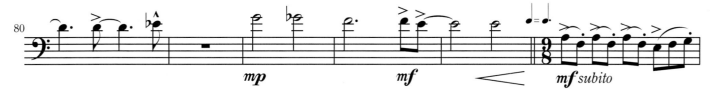

Trombone

# Amazing Grace

Trombone

# William Tell Overture

## MUSIC MINUS ONE
50 Executive Boulevard
Elmsford, New York 10523-1325
1.800.669.7464 (U.S.)/914.592.1188 (International)

www.musicminusone.com
e-mail: info@musicminusone.com

*Einojuhani*
# RAUTAVAARA

# *Hammarskjöld*
## FRAGMENT

för manskör
for male choir

CL 53
Chorus
SARJA
SERIES

I pris i Sällskapet MM:s nordiska kompositionstävling 1975